Jedi Manual Basic:
Introduction to Jedi Knighthood

Matthew T. Vossler

Copyright © 2009 by Matthew T. Vossler
Published by Dreamz-Work Productions, LLC
All Rights Reserved

Jedi is a trademarked name used by George Lucas referencing his characters in the Star Wars movies and stories. My use of Jedi in this manual refers specifically and only to those practitioners of Jediism, the official religion in the country of Canada.

This handbook is for individual use only. The unauthorized reproduction, distribution or sale of this material, including electronic reproductions is strictly prohibited. Please contact the publisher at matovo@comcast.net for information regarding possible exceptions to this provision.

Dreamz-Work Productions, LLC
4306 Independence Street
Rockville, MD 20853
USA
www.dreamz-work.com

ISBN 978-0-9825531-2-1
First edition: October 2009
Printed in the United States of America

Description:

This manual introduces the requirements for becoming a Jedi Knight. You will be given some examples of how others have accomplished this and what it means to be a Knight. I will assign projects that can be considered basic "tests" along your path to becoming a Jedi Knight with the goal of ultimately becoming a master.

The manual will also cover some Jedi philosophy, religious aspects, and hands-on techniques that Jedi Knights can use. In this regard, the manual acts as a pointer to other resources available for further investigation and work.

The assignments provided at the end of lessons 2 through 7 are not mandatory, but they are recommended and are designed so that you will get the most out of studying the material. Use the space available in the text for the assignments or create a journal to complete the essays.

CONTENTS:

1. INTRODUCTION
2. WHAT IT MEANS TO BE A KNIGHT
3. BECOMING A KNIGHT
4. JEDI PHILOSOPHY AND RELIGION
5. SCIENTIFIC BACKING
6. DEALING WITH SITH AND OTHER PRACTICAL APPLICATIONS
7. CONCLUSION

Additional Materials:

Access to the Internet

1. INTRODUCTION

"Try not. Do, or do not. There is no try"
- *Master Yoda*

After working through this manual, you should know the following:

- Know what it means to be a Knight and specifically a Jedi Knight.
- How to begin to apply the lessons of Knighthood in your modern life.
- Some of the Jedi philosophy and teachings
- Some of the options and avenues open to one interested in following the path of the Jedi Knight
- Some of the meditative techniques and energy work used by Jedi Knights

Additional Resources

The following links may be helpful as you

study the materials in this class:

- http://www.jediresourcecenter.org/?board=15.0
- http://www.jedisanctuary.org/forum/viewtopic.php?t=164
- http://psipog.net/home.html
- http://www.jediresourcecenter.org/?board=15.0
- http://www.marylandjedi.org
- http://www.completemartialarts.com
- http://www.orderofthejedi.ca/

Recommended Books:

- *The Power of Now* by Eckhart Tolle – Published by New World Library (September 29, 2004)

- *The Power of Intentions* by Dr. Wayne Dyer – Published by Hay House; 1 edition (December 15, 2005)

- *Open Heart, Clear Mind* by Thubten Chodron – Published by Snow Lion Publications; Later Printing edition (November 25, 1990)

- *Opening to Meditation: A Gentle, Guided Approach* by Diana Lang – Published by New World Library (Hardcover - Oct 31, 2004)

- Any Star Wars literature (for teachings of the Jedi)

Recommended Movies:

- Any Star Wars Movie (for teachings of the Jedi)

2. WHAT IT MEANS TO BE A KNIGHT

What is a Jedi Knight?

George Lucas invented the term Jedi Knight. In the Star Wars movie series and the numerous books and websites they spawned, the Jedi Knight has become famous as guardians and protectors of the people. They have special powers to manipulate energy, or "The Force," and they brandish high-tech light sabers to accomplish their noble goals.

Real world Jedi Knights accomplish their goals and purpose not with a sword or light-saber, but with calm debate, the pen, or any number of peaceful techniques, including energy manipulation. But a Jedi can also take advantage of technology to create a better world.

An example of how a real world Jedi Knight can use technology (rather than a fictional light-saber) is by brandishing a cell phone; yes, a cell phone! Today most cell phones can take pictures and video.

Modern Jedi have broken up or prevented fights and other bad deeds by calling attention to the fact that they are video-taping what is going on. Whether they are actually filming or not, just holding up the phone and pointing it at the situation can sometimes make a big difference in the outcome of a bad situation. I have personally broken up one fight between two young men using this technique and prevented a potential fight on another occasion.

It is good to exercise caution though, even if you are a bystander taking video. This technique is not recommended for readers who are under 18 years of age or for anyone who deems the situation too dangerous for them to stand by and watch. It may be better to use the cell phone to call authorities for assistance.

To help us learn more about what it means to be a Jedi Knight, let's take a tour of the origins and meaning of knighthood in human history. A good place to start is the dictionary.

According to dictionary.com, a knight is one "bound to chivalrous conduct."

One having chivalry is courageous, honorable, and loyal. They would also be gracious, considerate, and gallant. A female knight is sometimes called a Dame.

The idea of the knight has been with us for at least as long as recorded history. The tale of King Arthur and the Knights of the Round Table and similar myths are woven into the fabric of our human psyche. The idea of a journey to find the Holy Grail is that of the knight in search of the true meaning of life and his or her purpose. The grail holds what some traditions call the living water, or water of life; enlightenment and bliss.

Perhaps this meaning is different for each of us, but then again, maybe it is the same for all of us.

An Ideal Jedi Knight

An ideal Jedi Knight would certainly be chivalrous as defined above. A Jedi Knight is also someone who serves and puts others before her or himself. A Jedi Knight would be true to a higher cause or mission, but at the same time would follow the laws of their land or origin. A Jedi is humble, but humility is often misunderstood. It is not humiliation or just to eat humble pie; to be humble is to acknowledge truth.

Albert Einstein when asked, "Are you a genius like they say?" He answered, "Yes, thank God!" Although Einstein acknowledged his greatness of mind, ego did not play a part in this case, as he was only stating the truth. This is humility.

A Jedi Knight will know what is just and what is not just, but understands that this determination is different for each individual, to a greater or lesser degree.

To defend the innocent is just, but it is not just to do so in a cruel way. Force is reserved for when other options are exhausted, and one's foe is not to be destroyed, but to be rendered harmless and then rehabilitated if possible.

In Sum:

A Jedi Knight is courageous, dauntless, valiant, courtly; faithful, true, and devoted. Someone who serves others, leads by good example and upholds high standards defined by true integrity. A good measure for a Jedi Knight is to interfere in other's affairs only when they are unjustly harming others or have intentions to do so. Ultimately, a Jedi is a hero.

A Jedi Knight <u>is not</u> cowardly, cruel, discourteous, disloyal, crude, or weak. He or she is not one to seek power for the sake of power or vainglory.

Reading Assignment (the only one for this manual)

Go to the following websites or similar ones and read about the knight in medieval history and some of the famous knights of history.

http://www.historicalweapons.com/knights.html ,
http://www.britainexpress.com/History/Knights_and_Fights.htm ,
http://www.angelfire.com/mi4/polcrt/KnightsTemplar1.html , and
http://library.thinkquest.org/TQ0313002/Medieval/famous.html

When you are ready, please complete the following (optional)

Essay #1:

Based on the reading assignment and any other research, describe in approximately 700 words the history of the medieval knight, the knightly code, and examples of some knights of history. Is a knight someone who always lives up to the standards set for them?

Also research the story of King Arthur and the Knights of the Round Table. Describe how the ideas of freedom and equality in this tale are interwoven into the idea of the knight and knightly behavior.

_____

_____

_____

_____

_____

_____

_____

_____

_____

_____

_____

3. BECOMING A KNIGHT

Modern Knights and Jedi Knighthood

How does one become a Jedi Knight? There is a knight or dame in each of us waiting to come out. To become a Jedi Knight, one trains either formally or informally by life experience. Both are effective, although training through life and the school of hard knocks often takes longer.

A Jedi Knight can be a healer, warrior (peacekeeper), or teacher; indeed, they can be any profession as long they are committed to improving themselves, the conditions around them, and passing on what wisdom they can to those who are agreeable to learning.

A Jedi Knight can be religious or not. Jediism has something for everyone. If you are not particularly religious, but spiritually-minded, there are many Jedi groups that focus on the practical, hands-on aspects of ideas such as martial arts and energy work. If you don't call yourself spiritual, the overlaps between Jediism and science can be interesting. If you are religious in nature, there are groups that focus on Jediism as a religion. See:

http://www.orderofthejedi.org

Some key words for those interested in the Jedi path are: healing, martial arts, service, psychic awareness, peace making, faith, personal path, growth, tolerance, philosophy, and self control.

Jedi or Jedi Knights follow the laws of the land, serve others, and strive to do and be what is right and good. Jedi also teach their wisdom to those curious and agreeable to learning, growing, and serving.

Formal Training

Training to become a Jedi involves time and several steps, some of which can be done congruently. Dedication to sustained effort is required and the decision to begin training is not to be made lightly.

This manual offers an outline and some exercises for beginning such training and acts as a pointer to further resources for those who wish to go on to higher levels of mastery.

Training to be a Jedi Knight includes the following paths. Each path leads to the final path, the goal of a Jedi Knight. A Jedi can choose to focus on one or more of these at any given time. A Jedi is a master if they achieve mastery in one or more of the 12 paths.

The 12 Paths of a Jedi Knight

- Training and practice in meditation
- Training and practice in martial arts (specifically)

- Training and practice in the healing arts
- Training and practice in psychic awareness and social graces
- Training and practice in mediation, diplomacy, and peacemaking
- Training and practice in the Jedi philosophy and religion
- Training and practice in teaching, coaching, and mentoring
- Training and practice in practical skills for defending and protecting others
- Training and practice in gentle and objective deliberation, persuasion, and debate
- Training and practice in literary and theatrical arts
- Training and practice in working with energy and the supernatural
- Sustained pursuit of knowledge and wisdom and attaining a good measure thereof

The goal: To use one or more of these masteries to better serve others.

Modern day examples of higher profile Jedi Knights are the police and firefighters who rescued people after the 9/11 disaster at the World Trade Center in New York City, disaster relief workers who left their homes and families and traveled to New Orleans to help those whose lives were devastated by Hurricane Katrina, doctors who travel to developing countries to give healing aid to so many who have little or nothing, religious leaders like the Dalai Lama, and Hollywood stars like Angelina Jolie who use their stardom and resources to help others and make the world a better place.

This is a very short list. I cannot possibly give all the examples of modern day Jedi. In addition to the high profile knights, there are many heroes who don't make the headlines but practice one or more of the paths every day. Examples of these kinds of Jedi are the mom who sacrifices her own dinner so her children can eat, the minister of the local church or circle who helps families struggle with the heartache of loosing a loved one, the social worker who helps drug addicts turn their lives around, and the inner city teacher who, against all odds, inspires their students to greatness.

Not all of these people have trained for knighthood. Some have trained formally in professions and some by the experiences of life, but all give of themselves while asking little in return. All are heroes, not just for a day, but consistently over time; they can be counted on.

Is this what you aspire to? Think hard. If so, then make a decision. A true decision means to cut off all other possibilities. As Master Yoda says, *"Try not. Do, or do not. There is no try."*

The decision is to dedicate your life to one of service, to put aside your self in pursuit of a higher purpose. How will you know if you are following the right path? You'll know, and you'll also realize when you have fallen away from it, too. There will come a time when the pain of not following your path is too painful to not do what is right and true for very long. Be glad because this is a good thing, and it means that you are on your way to mastery.

Will it always be easy? No. Will people always understand and love you? No. Will you make a better life for yourself and others? Most definitely!

When you are ready, please complete the following (optional)

Essay #2:

Think about what it means to be of service to others. Decide how you can be of service to others in a way that you are not already practicing or doing. Make it something significant. Some examples are volunteering at a soup kitchen or in an animal shelter, or tutoring at school. Do it for one to two weeks. Keep a journal of your experience. How did it make you feel? Was it hard to put yourself aside and others first? What impact do you think you made on others by doing this? Is this something you think you will continue in the future? What did you learn about yourself from this? What did you learn about others from this?

4. JEDI PHILOSOPHY AND RELIGION

The Force:

George Lucas wrote about an ancient religion, at the center of which is a belief in something called The Force. "May the Force be with you," is a line that is used many times in Lucas' Star Wars saga.

"There is one all powerful force that binds the entire universe together. It is an energy field created by all living things. It surrounds us, penetrates us, and binds the galaxy together." --George Lucas.

To many modern day Jedi, The Force is an impersonal energy source. It is also the intelligence that set all things in place and motion along with the natural and spiritual laws. It is in us, of us, and through us, as well as all things in the universe. It is energy, it is intelligence, it is love, and it is eternal.

The Jedi Code:

Many groups and religions live by an established and accepted code of conduct and/or code of ethics. Much has been written and talked about regarding the Jedi Code. In a work subsequent to the Star Wars movie series, the following code of the Jedi has become very popular. From: http://starwars-exodus.wikia.com/wiki/Jedi_Order

"The Jedi Code as was rewritten by Grand Master Luke Skywalker upon reestablishing the Jedi Order in the Galaxy:

- Jedi are the guardians of peace in the galaxy.

- Jedi use their powers to defend and to protect.

- Jedi respect all life, in any form.

- Jedi serve others rather than ruling over them, for the good of the galaxy.

- Jedi seek to improve themselves through knowledge and training."

More on Jedi Philosophy:

A Jedi or Jedi Knight is an ideal that one can strive for. A Jedi always wants to become better or improve him or herself. Being a Jedi Master means that you are committed to improving yourself, the conditions around you and passing on what wisdom you can to those who are agreeable to learning.

A Jedi is someone who always strives for more but is not overly attached to outcomes. At the idealistic level, a Jedi has no attachments in this world, and in that respect, the Jedi path is similar to the Buddhist philosophy and goal. In practicality, a Jedi lives according to the middle way, by embracing both the physical/material world and the spiritual nature of reality.

Also, to be a Jedi Knight is to have a reverence for and devotion to an aspect of reality that requires a leap of faith. Science has not yet proved or disproved the existence of an all pervasive, intelligent, life-energy within the fabric of reality: A force that binds the universe and all things together, one that guides and teaches, nurtures and honors, loves and sustains. One that surrounds us, comes from us, flows through us and is our true selves. But a Jedi knows these things to be true!

A Jedi strives to come from a place of detachment, and because of love, will take actions to defend, protect, and help others. A Jedi can be detached from the things of this world because she or he knows that death is not really death, but an opportunity to transform into the Living Force. To be detached is to be aware that all is interconnected and whole at the basic level. Love is the realization of this; to feel the presence of the one life beneath all life. Without detachment there is no awareness of true love, and it is out of love that a Jedi finds their purpose.

A Jedi has a seriousness of mind that comes with wisdom. He or she has a respect for all life. Out of this respect and love for life, a Jedi has the disposition to protect and help others.

A Jedi believes that she or he can ask or draw upon the Living Force at any time and what a person does with the power is a matter of choice. In this respect the Force can be understood as an impersonal energy source. But many believe that it is more than that.

The faith itself can be a source of comfort and helps a Jedi to hold her or himself to a high standard. Such a standard is somewhat subjective, as is much in this world. A Jedi knows that every person has the understanding of what ultimately is right and wrong. In this respect, Jedi are not moral relativists.

The Force is known by other names such as the Source or Source of Life, The Light, God, Goddess, Chi, Lord, Lady, Kundalini, Zeus, Odin, Isis, Allah, Aphrodite, and many others. The Force allows us to make choices and make mistakes. It does not interfere, but lets us find out for ourselves what is right or wrong based on the natural order of things including negative or positive consequences of our individual and collective actions.

We are all destined to return to the Force at the end of our journey. When we return, we are whole and in a state of bliss. Master Yoda stated in the third Star Wars episode, "Rejoice for those around you who transform into The Force."

Jediism as a Religion:

All religions have at their core a body of literature; stories told either by oral tradition or through the written word or other media. Jediism is no different in this respect. Like the Sun, which existed before people gave it a name, modern Jedi see their beliefs grounded in truths that were here before the popular movies put a name to them. It is only natural that many spiritually-minded people would resonate with and follow the notions put forth in the works of George Lucas.

When you are ready, please complete the following (optional)

Essay #3:

In 500 words, describe your understanding of the Jedi philosophy and religion. Do you agree or disagree with it? Why or why not?

_____

_____

_____

_____

_____

_____

_____

_____

_____

5. SCIENTIFIC BACKING

Science, and particularly, quantum physics and cosmology, seems to be bearing out the idea of The Force. Scientists are finding that the universe is connected at the fundamental level by energy. While much is theoretical and unproven, each year more evidence is uncovered to support these ideas. The following is an introduction for those who may wish to investigate further modern scientific support of Jedi beliefs.

Science, String Theory, and Jedi Mysticism

String theory came about in an attempt to find one theory for everything in the universe. It was one of Einstein's great ambitions, which he didn't get to finish. Those who came after him built upon it. String Theory is what was developed and it proposes that the fundamental building blocks of matter are microscopic filaments of vibrating energy that are in the shape of a string, millions of times smaller than electrons, protons, and neutrons.

This theory takes the idea of our three-dimensional world plus time (equals four dimensions) and mathematically and conceptually adds six more dimensions. These extra dimensions are microscopic in size so we cannot perceive them. After a while of studying string theory, physicists ran into a problem. They found that there were really five string theories and they could not mathematically account for these theories existing among themselves simultaneously.

Meanwhile, there was another theory making a sensation in the scientific circles called Super Gravity theory. This theory accounted for a total of ten dimensions plus time, and that meant according to this theory there are 11 dimensions in total.

The string theorists grabbed on to this and did some math. This was a very exciting time within the community, for the physicists believed that they might finally be onto a unified theory of everything. This 11th dimension was seen by the string theorists as a way to unite the five different string theories and make sense of them. The result was something called M theory, where M stands for membrane. It now appears that the universe is not only made up of strings of vibrating energy, but the strings are all woven together like a giant quilt or membrane.

So this means that the fundamental makeup of our universe; space time and every thing that is called matter, is energy. Big surprise, huh? Since this energy vibrates in different frequencies accounting for the diversity of matter around us, the implications are kind of profound. What we call Jedi mysticism is continually being proven by science.

So when someone tells you that Jedi mysticism is nothing but foolishness, ask them if they realize that there is more *not* there than is there to the chair they sit on. For this is true; there is vastly more space between all the electrons, protons, and neutrons that make up a chair than there is of the any real material. Then they might ask, what's the matter with you? And you would answer, "Exactly! What's the matter with me is really all energy." At this point I am sure that you have lost them, but probably some day they will get it and much more than that!

References:

- Parallel Universes, Retrieved on 10/29/08 from: http://www.youtube.com/watch?v=gWIyam5cAko&feature=PlayList&p=229C082DB5FEA79F&index=0
- Hawking, S. & Mlodinow, L. *A Briefer History of Time*, Bantam (2008)
- Greene, B. *The Fabric of the Cosmos: Space, Time, and the Texture of Reality*, Vintage (2005)

When you are ready, please complete the following (optional)

Essay #4:

In about 500 words, answer the following. Do you think that current science supports the idea of The Force? Do you think that science is moving in the direction of supporting even more the idea that we are all connected in an essential way by a living Force? Why or why not?

6. DEALING WITH SITH AND OTHER PRACTICAL APPLICATIONS

"Fear is a path to the dark side. Fear leads to anger, anger leads to hate, hate leads to suffering." -- Master Yoda, Star Wars, Episode One.

According to George Lucas, The Force has both a light side and a dark side. This idea is found in most religions under various names. In Christianity it refers to the ideas of heaven and hell; in Eastern thought, it is referred to as Yin and Yang or negative and positive.

In Star Wars, those who embrace the dark side of The Force are called Sith. The main difference between Sith and Jedi are that Jedi strive to serve others, while Sith strive to be served by others, to rule with complete power. Jedi are devoted to democracy and human rights, while Sith wish to control completely without regard to the individual.

In our human history, Adolph Hitler could be considered a Sith Lord. One can also encounter Sith in their daily lives. Someone who is usually positive in nature can become Sith-like for a time. This doesn't mean that your boyfriend or girlfriend, mother or father are Siths because they break a promise or say something hurtful, but it is a small taste of what the dark side of the Force can do; its power can draw any of us in. We all have a dark side to our nature, whether we admit it or not. It is our choice to feed it and give it power and strength.

How do Jedi deal with Sith and the dark side of The Force?

Some techniques for dealing with Sith:

(For the purposes of this manual, Sith refers only to the fictional concept created by George Lucas)

With the exception of a physical assault, etc., there is an old saying: "What is the sound of one hand clapping?" Meaning that to start something, it takes two. If someone wants to start something (a dispute or argument) and they are ignored, it is like trying to clap with one hand; it goes nowhere!

When you are assaulted verbally or emotionally techniques of verbal self defense can and should be used. The book, "*The Gentle Art of Verbal Self-Defense,*" by Suzette Haden Elgin, is a great resource for learning these skills. I highly recommend this book for anyone, for we all encounter Sith from time to time and some of us deal with the assault of the dark side on a daily basis.

It is important for Jedi to know that when we are having a strong emotional reaction to something or someone by what they say or do, it is a time to pay attention. Our reaction gives us vital clues about ourselves. On the other hand, when someone says something hurtful to you, often it says more about them than about you. But remember that our feelings in general give us information that can be useful in knowing what to do or about who we are right now.

Another way to deal with Sith-like behavior in others is to use the power of positive thinking. Expect other(s) in your life to be better. Do this purposefully and often. It is hard to sustain this, but refuse to give in to hate and negativity. Keep expecting the best in others and in life, and after a while this is what will show up for you more and more.

Once this starts to happen, it is hard to stop and the cycle has reversed from negative to positive. You can begin this practice at any time. If you falter, you can restart it anytime. What you have gained will likely not be lost. Giving in temporally is only natural, but to believe that this is permanent is self-defeating and a lie.

Meditation: A Staple of Jedi Life and Training

Living in the now is essential for Jedi. Being completely present is rarely achieved and when it is done you will recognize it immediately. It is like no other experience you can imagine. A good way to bring more presence into your life and consciousness is by practicing meditation.

Meditation is one of the most effective tools that a Jedi can use. I cannot stress this enough. It is through meditation that a Jedi learns to be at peace with him or herself. Meditation teaches patience and objectivity, essential to mastery of life.

There are many classes, books, and websites devoted to meditation. Because of this, I will not teach meditation in this manual, but the following are some key points to remember about the practice and its benefits:

Meditation is a technique for calming and stilling your mind and spirit so that you become more present in your life. Meditation allows one to become more fully alive and to live in the now. Living your life in the now is a more timeless state of being that opens the door to deeper meanings.

Things to note:

- Ultimately there is no right or wrong way to meditate
- Meditation benefits are cumulative
- Some of your meditation sessions will have better results than others. This is normal and it doesn't mean failure if every session doesn't put you into a trance or relax your mind and body.
- You don't lose the benefits you've gained, even after a break in practice.

Benefits of meditation:

- Relaxation
- Healing
- Becoming one with your true self
- Gateway to more awareness in your life and better intuition
- Create a stronger spiritual connection
- Better health
- Becoming more present and aware
- To know yourself better

Mastery for a Jedi - A Meditation on Self Improvement and Creating a Better Life:

In order to create and bring lasting fulfillment in your life, you need to create/remember the skills to live in the now, to be fully present within yourself always. As you do this, all lasting change will come to you automatically. You will no longer be controlled by ego and trapped by the illusion of time, continuously repenting the past and mulling the future. You will enjoy the experience of pure being and can live by the middle way, neither trying to completely deny your physical body and world, nor shunning your spiritual, un-manifested reality of being God/Spirit/Energy/Light/Life/**Force**.

As this happens, everything you could possibly want and things you didn't know you wanted will be realized in your life. Some things you may think you wanted will no longer hold any appeal. Your life will turn from a dull agitated series of habitual running from this thing to that, never being satisfied and being tormented by compulsive thinking, to a life of wholeness, joy and satisfaction.

This is all you really need to have happen in your life, although it isn't easy to bring one's self to this point of living in the here and now 100 percent. This is called the awakened state or enlightenment or salvation if you will. All else will fall into place quickly and easily as this happens. You will have lasting fulfillment and will be fully in touch with the being of life; you will be Life/Divinity/Force itself, at one with all life, dwelling in the realm of pure Spirit.

How do you make this happen in your life? Easier Said than Done...

Begin to accomplish this by practicing being body conscious by focusing on your physical body and the body within – the spiritual body or light body. Remember that the physical body is a thin veil through which we can experience the divine whole. And this is our true self. Practice meditation every day or as often as possible.

Observe what your thoughts are and remember that past and future do not exist; only the now exists. Learn to control the mind, not the reverse. Observe your inner feelings often, and what is going on inside you.

(Source Material: Some of the ideas in this meditation are derived from Eckhart Tolle's, "The Power of Now")

When you are ready, please complete the following (optional)

Essay #5:

In about 500 words, describe how you might deal with someone insulting you unfairly? Would your reaction be in keeping with Jedi teachings on how to react? Give an example of a time when you *did* live up to the Jedi standards in this regard, and an example of when you did not live up to the standards.

The next time you are faced with a Sith or Sith like behavior in your life, try to stop and remember the lessons in this class and to modify your reactions using one or more of the tools of the Jedi to make the situation better or even corrected completely.

_____

_____

_____

_____

_____

_____

_____

_____

_____

_____

7. CONCLUSION

We've learned about the idea of the knight in our human history and human experience. We've learned what it means to be a Jedi Knight and what their purpose is. We've begun to learn what it takes to be a Jedi and hopefully you have made progress in finding out whether or not this path is for you.

The science of Jediism has been lightly touched on, and some of the practical techniques such as meditation, knowing yourself, being present, dealing with the dark side, have been introduced.

The material here is a beginning to what could be a change of life for you. To become a person of service and to transform from a more self-centered existence to a more selfless one leads to a better life for you and our world.

To hold yourself to a higher standard, to be a protector and respecter of all life, and defender of the best aspects of civilization is an important vocation to take on. The decision to take the path of the Jedi is a serious one. It means a life committed to self analysis and improvement. To sustain a life of service and non-violence, both physically and verbally, is a tall order.

To be a Jedi Knight is to be a hero. It is a path to mastery. A Master Jedi Knight is a rare gift to humanity, a crown jewel, and a vital piece to the health and survival of human civilization.

I hope you will consider joining the Jedi Order to make a difference in your life and those around you by taking the path of the Jedi Knight!
When you are ready, please complete the following final essay (optional)

Final Essay

I have reproduced below the list of paths from lesson three that lead to the goal of a Jedi Knight. Choose any two of these paths and write an 800 word (approx) essay on how you would follow the paths if you chose to become a Master Jedi Knight. How would you determine mastery of them? How would you use such skills in achieving the goal of a Jedi Knight?

The 12 Paths of a Jedi Knight:

- *Training and practice in meditation*
- *Training and practice in martial arts (specifically)*
- *Training and practice in the healing arts*
- *Training and practice in psychic awareness and social graces*
- *Training and practice in mediation, diplomacy, and peacemaking*
- *Training and practice in the Jedi philosophy and religion*
- *Training and practice in teaching, coaching, and mentoring*
- *Training and practice in practical skills for defending and protecting others*
- *Training and practice in gentle and objective deliberation, persuasion, and debate*
- *Training and practice in literary and theatrical arts*

- *Training and practice in working with energy and the supernatural*
- *Sustained pursuit of knowledge and wisdom and attaining a good measure thereof*

The goal: *To use one or more of these masteries to better serve others.*

_____

_____

_____

_____

_____

_____

_____

_____

_____

Congratulations on completing the Jedi Manual Basic. I hope you found it interesting and enlightening. We are hard at work developing the Jedi Manual Intermediate.

May the Light of the Force guide you and be with you always!

Appendix A

In Support of the Force:

Here are some thoughts from Allen L. Roland, PhD.

On the Consciousness of Matter:

"Where Einstein was concerned with the *without* of things, like time and space, Teilhard de Chardin was concerned with the *within* of things.

Teilhard used the term within to denote the psychic face or consciousness of matter ~ since the beginning of time ~ which reveals itself in its innate urge to unite.

Teilhard defines this innate urge to unite as an energy force in his famous Law of Complexity - Consciousness.

The law states two principles:

1. Throughout all time there has been an evolutionary tendency for all matter to unite and become increasingly complex in nature.

2. With each increase in material complexity, there is a related rise in the consciousness of matter and an even greater urge to unite.

Teilhard divided this fundamental energy into two distinct components ~ a Tangential energy which linked the element with all others of the same order and a Radial energy which represented the innate urge toward union and greater complexity as well as a leap in consciousness.

Teilhard foresaw in the 1950's the eventual emergence of the NOOSPHERE where all minds would be connected and all information would be instantly available to anyone on the planet.

As such, he has often been called the true spiritual father of the Internet where all of this is currently taking place. But very few people are aware that Teilhard also saw the emergence of the NOOSPHERE as a prelude to the SOULOSPHERE ~ where all hearts would be connected through social cooperation and altruism."

"The basic underlying and uniting force of the universe is a psychic energy field of love and soul consciousness (the Unified Field) which lies not only beyond time and space but ALSO beneath our deepest fears."

-Allen L. Roland, PhD

Allen's Website:
http://www.allenroland.com/allen.php

Appendix B

On Service to Life and Humankind

Leveraging efforts when facilitating societal change

By Master Zindel of the Maryland Jedi Order

For greater success in recruiting and making positive changes in your community and world, identify areas that could be called "arteries." These are pressure points, or in political terms, swing states. This could mean identifying an area where there is a great need for change, and concentrating efforts there, or identifying the type of person who would be receptive to a particular cause.

It might mean identifying a place where there are many such people or an area known as a trend setter (Celebrities often have trend setting power, as well). By such discerning, recruiting efforts and action measures can be leveraged for better success. Here are some other tips:

When talking to others, get them to talk about what interests them, rather than just talking to them. This is a basic sales technique, and a good communication technique, period.

Flyers are best for posting on community bulletin boards and such, while business cards are best for handing out to people as they pass. Cards are more apt to be accepted as they are easily put into a pocket, billfold, pocketbook or backpack. Be sure to have a web-site URL and/or other contact information on the card along with a tag line that peeks interest and encourages one to go to the site or investigate further.

Have a vision for what you want to accomplish, but don't become overly attached to results. Being too attached to results can get frustrating because it is often hard to see your impact right away. You might be doing much more good than you know, even if the results are delayed for weeks months or years.

Visualize success in your efforts, take action, and observe the results objectively. Learn from your experience and keep at it, tweaking methods based on what you have learned.

Relax, have fun and enjoy life! - This is contagious, and why not bring joy to the process?

The Assist Card is a new program for the Maryland Jedi Order. This idea was handed down to us by the Order of the Jedi, Canada. An assist card is a calling card which we would leave anonymously after performing some form of community service. (See example assist card on the next page).

Example of an assist card on following page:

A helping hand was provided by,
a member of the:

Order of the Jedi Canada

www.orderofthejedi.ca

**Commited to teaching solid values,
through strong moral and ethical guidance**

Appendix C

Wisdom from the Jedi Universe

"Jedi are peacemaker's, protectors, and respecters of life in the world/universe. We strive to serve rather than rule. Self and societal improvement is our cause. We recognize and accept that people have different views of life, faith, and meaning."

--Maryland Jedi Order

"No Jedi would be a true devotee who didn't question the system, along with everything else."

--Obi-Wan Kenobi, The Approaching Storm

"The greatest harm lies in doing nothing."

--Luke Skywalker, Fate of the Jedi – Abyss

"Never" means the right opportunity has not yet arisen."

--Bothan saying, X-Wing – The Krytos Trap

"Curiosity is the sign of intelligence."

--Boss, Republic Commando – True Colors

"There's nothing wrong with feeling and acknowledging sorrow and pain…The crime is letting them hold you prisoner."

--Jula Darklighter , X-Wing – The Bacta War

"Opportunity rarely comes without risk."

--5YQ, Coruscant Nights – Patterns of the Force

"There is no shame in admitting one does not know everything. It shows wisdom. That is a much more valued talent than physical strength—or even the ability to influence the Force. You are to be commended, not condemned."

--Luminara Unduli, The Approaching Storm

"Pride is pretty sneaky, it disguises it-self pretty well."

--Jacen Solo, New Jedi Order – Edge of Victory I Conquest

"When are cowardz not threatened by the brave?"

--Saba Sebatyne, New Jedi Order – Star by Star

"No wall can contain the Force."

--Luke Skywalker, Luke Skywalker and the Shadows of Mindor

"Cuteness should be preserved."

--Ton Phanan, X-Wing – Iron Fist

"Potential that goes unrealized is potential that might as well not exist in the first place."

--Barriss Offee, The Approaching Storm

"Knowledge was like that — once it was ushered into the light, putting it back into the shadows was difficult, if not impossible."

--Atour Riten, Death Star

The Combat Litany of the Smuggler's Creed

*"Never fight when you can bluff.
Never bluff when you can run.
Never run when you can sneak.
If no one knows you're there, you win."*

--Luke Skywalker and the Shadows of Mindor

"Teaching trust is a long process; learning it an even longer one."

--Kirtan Loor, X-Wing – The Krytos Trap

"Desperation fuels inspiration."

--Borsk Fey'lya, X-Wing – Isard's Revenge

"Only those of us who have been slaves can really taste freedom."

--Anakin Skywalker, Jedi Quest – The Way of the Apprentice

"Freedom is always alarming."

--Vergere, New Jedi Order – Traitor

"Honor exists inside you and can only radiate out. What goes on outside can't change it or kill it unless you abandon your honor. Too many folks give it up too easily, then do whatever it takes to fill the void in their hearts."

--Tycho Celchu, X-Wing – Rogue Squadron

"Pain can be power, too. Power to change things for the better. That's how change happens: Someone hurts, and sooner or later decides to do something about it. Suffering is the fuel in the engine of civilization."

--Jacen Solo, New Jedi Order – Traitor

"Those who have their mouths open all the time generally have their ears shut."

--Barriss Offee; The Approaching Storm

"The chink in the armor of powerful beings was that they believed power made them smarter, as well as blaster proof."

--Atour Riten; Death Star

"Don't waste time worrying about what should be. Worry about what is."

--Aeona Cantor, Luke Skywalker and the Shadows of Mindor

"Evil compounds exponentially."

--Mrlssi saying, Death Star

"When to the Force you truly give yourself, all you do expresses the truth of who you are. Then through you the Force will flow, and guide your hand it will, until the greatest good might come of your smallest gesture."

--Yoda, Luke Skywalker and the Shadows of Mindor

"I know myself to be only as I appear to myself."

--Jhaveek, Death Star

"Gone is the past, he remembered Master Yoda saying once. Imaginary is the future. Always now, even eternity will be. Which Luke had always interpreted as Don't worry about what's already done, and don't worry about what you'll do later. Do something now."

--Yoda and Luke Skywalker, Luke Skywalker and the Shadows of Mindor

"Anyone can handle a weapon. Reason is much more difficult to wield. Remember that the next time you're tempted to settle an argument with a lightsaber."

--Luminara Unduli, The Approaching Storm

"If far from the Force you find yourself, trust you can that it is not the Force that moved."

--Yoda; Luke Skywalker and the Shadows of Mindor

"Sometimes, things not going according to plan is a gift."

--Han Solo; Luke Skywalker and the Shadows of Mindor

"My commitment to others had to be total and complete. I was an agent of life every day, every hour, every second; for as long as I lived, and then some."

--Corran Horn, I, Jedi

"Every living species in the galaxy knows that one either adapts or dies."

--Jax Pavan, Coruscant Nights – Street of Shadows

"Comfort was always easier to steal than to earn, peace easier to break than to keep."

--Leia Organa Solo; New Jedi Order – Star by Star

"Caution is admirable, but do not let it be a barrier to a greater truth."

--Elegos A'Kla, I, Jedi

NOTES:

NOTES:

NOTES:

NOTES:

NOTES:

Dreamz-Work Productions, LLC